"What I Know About the Old Ways"

by Agnes Vanderburg

"What I Know About the Old Ways"

The Life and Wisdom of a Flathead Indian Reservation Elder

by Agnes Vanderburg

published by
Salish Kootenai College Press
Pablo, Montana

distributed by
University of Nebraska Press
Lincoln, Nebraska

2022

Cover illustration:
Agnes Vanderburg. Photo taken by Clarence Woodcock. Courtesy Séliš–Qlispé Culture Committee,St. Ignatius, Montana

Library of Congress Cataloging-in-Publication Data:
Names: Vanderburg, Agnes, 1901-1989, author.
Title: "What I know about the old ways" : the life and wisdom of a Flathead Indian Reservation elder / by Agnes Vanderburg.
Other titles: Life and wisdom of a Flathead Indian Reservation elder
Description: Pablo, Montana : Salish Kootenai College Press, [2022] | Includes bibliographical references and index.
Identifiers: LCCN 2022031131 | ISBN 9781934594322 (paperback)
Subjects: LCSH: Vanderburg, Agnes, 1901-1989, author. | Salish Indians. | Salish women--Montana--Biography. | Older Salish Indians--Montana--Flathead Indian Reservation--Biography. | Flathead Indian Reservation (Mont.)--Biography.
Classification: LCC E99.S2 V355 2022 | DDC 978.6004/9794350092 [B]--dc23/eng/20220707
LC record available at https://lccn.loc.gov/2022031131

published by
Salish Kootenai College Press
PO Box 70
Pablo, MT 59855

Distributed by
University of Nebraska Press,
1225 L Street, Suite 200
Lincoln, NE 68588-0630,
order 1-800-848-6224, www.nebraskapress.unl.edu.

Table of Contents

Agnes "Naqey" Adams Vanderburg

1901–1989:

Introduction

Agnes lived her life the only way she knew: never losing her Salish identity as a gentle warm Salish woman, wife, and mother to 14 children. Agnes had a big heart and was always willing to share traditional knowledge with anyone willing to listen and learn. Fluent in her Salish language, she was determined to teach the language along with arts and crafts. She passed along her expertise in making clothing, tepees, and the art of tanning hides to make various types of clothing and accessories. She taught the Salish language as well as the crafts.

Agnes' knowledge of traditional food preparation and plant medicines was very important to be handed down to generations yet to come. Agnes continued to gather and use these foods and basic medicinal plants throughout her life.

In the interview she gave to the *Parabola* magazine, "Coming Back Slow," which is included in this book, she talked about all the aspects of her being. She was a firm believer in education. She encouraged her children and grandchildren to seek higher education. She knew that was the way of the future which was different from hers.

Agnes loved her children, grandchildren, great-grandchildren, and siblings. She spoke highly of her elders whom she embraced as her teachers of Salish culture and tradition. Culture is a way of life for an entire society, such as codes of manner, dress, language, religion, rituals, art, ceremonies, and food. Agnes always stressed that culture is learned, shared, and must be preserved.

This book is a compilation of Agnes' life. May her gentle ways and happy smile always be a reminder to those learning and teaching their heritage.

Lucy Vanderburg

"We're from Valla Creek"

by Agnes Vanderburg

recorded and introduced by
Barbara Springer Beck

Agnes Vanderburg has extensive knowledge of the traditional ways of the Flathead culture and a willingness and desire to share this information. She is a competent speaker of both English and Salish. She has lived through and adjusted to times of great change for her tribe and people and continues to be an active educator in traditional ways. Agnes is the subject of this biography because of her dynamic personality, the reasons stated above and the fact that she represents a generation almost gone. I hope to present insight into how one woman has learned to operate successfully in both the Indian and white worlds, and show Agnes in the context of her own cultural milieu.

Agnes is a Flathead Salish woman who was educated in the traditional ways of her tribe. Her culture has had and continues to have constant contact with the dominant American culture. Agnes has grown up during times of great change for her tribe. She is now [1982] 81 years old and lives on the Flathead Reservation three miles south of Arlee, Montana. Her home is located on land that was originally part of her husband Jerome's parents' allotment. Their children live on adjacent land. Agnes, her siblings, and parents [the Adams] resided at Valley Creek, and in Arlee during her childhood. She has spent all her life residing in this region.

Mrs. Vanderburg is active in the tribe as a teacher of traditional ways. She currently teaches classes at the Community Center in St. Ignatius on "just about everything, you name it." She also spends several months a year at a camp where she encourages cultural awareness and people come to learn. Agnes participates in group therapy as a cultural consultant as well. The group addresses such issues as suicide, parenting, family violence, communication, education, assertiveness, and cultural identity. Gathering of groups has long been important to the Flathead traditional way of life so group discussion as a method of problem solving is harmonious with cultural tradition. The group tries to recognize and utilize their cultural characteristics and differences. Agnes has worked with many people researching and demonstrating old methods of food gathering and preparation. She has identified in Salishan different plants and camping sites. Agnes also travels regularly to represent her tribe at conferences and get-togethers.

The interaction during my meetings with Agnes followed a definite pattern. Upon my arrival at Agnes's house I was greeted warmly after which we would chat for several minutes. She asked general questions about my well-being and I reciprocated. We would then settle down on her sofa and or an adjacent chair. Our arrangement was sometimes dictated by proximity to an electrical outlet for my tape recorder. Once the recorder was turned on the discussion became more businesslike and Agnes much less frequently initiated conversation. In most cases she would address a general question of mine either briefly or at some length then pause until asked another. Because of this mode of operation, I was forced to take a larger role than I had anticipated in directing her narrative. During our discussions Agnes would often bead and at intervals light up a cigarette. She always wore her glasses, a print dress with shoes and stockings and a scarf over her hair. Her grey braids were long and tied together behind the neck which allowed them to fall gracefully over her shoulders. Her quiet yet warm way put me at ease immediately.

Family

We're from Valla [Valley] Creek. That's where I's born, in Valla Creek. Our huntin' ground is Seeley Lake, then over past. My dad find out he can lease his land and he leased it and we came down to Arlee. We stayed with my grandma. We farm and all that. He had that place where I's born leased to some people; how much money they get for a year I don't know.

My mom was Adelle, Adelle Kaltomee. She had sisters Katherine, Cecil, Agthaa, Louise and Ann. Then she had one brother Baptiste. None of 'ems livin', they're all gone. My dad was Adams, Eneas Adams. I think my dad was born in Stevensville, my mother was born there too. Jerome was born in Stevensville.

Mary Kaltomee was my grandma, my mother's mother. They didn't have no last names before she got married. She lived for a hundred and eleven I think, but she couldn't walk. She had all her teeth but they were just small. She can see and she can hear pretty good. She had her own tepee 'cause she had three kids and her husband died, but they took care of her like her wood and grub. My grandma did live in the Bitterroot. I'm full-blood 'cause all my relatives comes from Stevensville.

Never knew my dad's parents. When I was comin', my mother was still packin' me, my grandpa died. He was Abel Adams. I don't even know his wife either. It was when they first got married she died. I didn' get to know them. I had a picture of the first Adams, Abel Adams. There's a picture, a bunch of 'em standin' and sittin' down. He was laying in front.

I just got one brother and one sister [still living]. My sister lives in Valla Creek. My brother, he and his kids lives by Jocko church. His boy's got eight kids, that's the brother that stayed in Valla Creek. Another Adams he's in Ronan, he's just got one boy. Then the girls, they were Adams [Agnes' nieces] you know their maiden name. They each got, I don't know how many kids. There's one in Camas Prairie. I had [sisters] Harriet, Adeline, Felicity, Susie, Mary, they're all gone except Harriet. Then two brothers, well one is gone and one is around, Loomie Adams and Louie Adams.

I got Encas and Joe and Annie and Vic and Lucy [Agnes's children]. That's their school pictures on the wall. Vic ain' got no kids, he's not married. Joe went into the Navy. Vic went in the Army. Eneas' daughter she went in the Air Force, she's married;

Adeline Fyant, Adele Adams [Agnes' mother], Agnes and
Jerome Vanderburg during the early 1960s.
Courtesy Vanderburg family, Arlee, Montana

she's got one little girl. Alice, that's Eneas's woman, she's got three boys of her own and the four of 'em live in Valla Creek. She's still workin' there. He's stayin' here takin' care of the cows but he goes to see his old lady in Valla Creek.

Annie stays way up on the hillside [to the west]. She's got a man but she don' want to get married. It's their business whatever they want to do. If she's not happy she's got a chance to leave him. Lucy lives right over here. She's workin', teachin' over in St. Ignatius, shorthand, 'cause she took that. There's hardly anybody got that shorthand. I'm a great grandmother, I got two great grandchildren, two girls. The rest of 'em [grandchildren] are still going to school.

Jerome's mother and dad lived right down here, further than Lucy's house. See they us'ta farm this place, plow and put the grain in and fall come they cut it. They us'ta have that thrashin' machine they fed it with wood, a big pile 'a wood out there and somebody feedin' the engine, some guys stackin', and two guys throwin' the bales in there. Us'ta be a lot of men workin' just on that thrashin' machine. See all that straw fallin' can't go anywhere so there's a guy movin' straw. If they let it stack up that pipe'll get filled.

There's one Vanderburg here, right next house [see map]. That's Jerome's bother Alek. Right here by Lake County Lane a house right in the middle by that corner that's Jerome's sister Louise. There's jus' three of 'em, was jus' three of 'em. Now there's jus' two, Alek and Louise. This whole side, that's Alek Vanderburg and my boy Joe Vanderburg. This corner way over there, that's George Vanderburg, Lake County Lane, first lane to your left as you come in. This one belongs to Eneas and Vic.

Jerome's mother and dad, that's how we got this land. I got mine in Valla Creek, I trade mine, I sold mine. I bought this piece for all my kids. It goes just here to Finley Creek. Jerome's dad's house was right here in the field. There was a few houses here and there, all government houses.

Agnes' Children: Back row, left to right, Joe, Eneas, and Victor
Vanderburg. Front row, Anna and Lucy Vanderburg.
Courtesy Vanderburg family, Arlee, Montana

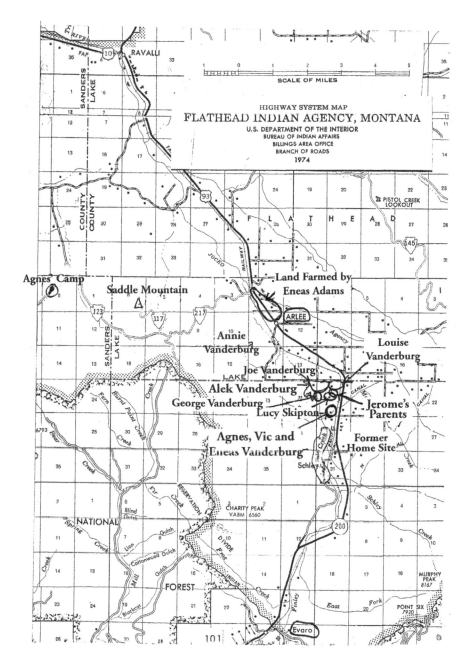

Vanderburg Family Residences, 1982

Vanderburg Name

The old ladies said nobody's white, it's just that Father gave 'em each last name. Then some people say, "Oh, you're German." I us'ta tell 'em no I'm not! It's just a name. That's what happened, 'cause they was gon' get baptized. Sack Woman and Jerome's dad's sister was tellin' us how it happened, 'cause they were there. She says we didn't know what two names mean [first and last names]. They didn't have no [last] name. Like Bear Tracks, that was his really name. When he was out there, [you say] hey Bear Track! that was him. Now, later after they got baptized, [you say] hey Louie Vanderburg! That's where Vanderburg came from was that priest. That's why that Vanderburg his name was Bear Track, his name wasn't Louie. They [the Indians] know everybody [by their Indian name]. My grandfather, my dad's dad, his beard was red and that's what they call him, he didn't have no name like Abel Adams. That's all they called him, was just by his beard. So the priest was the one that gave 'em all those names, like Abel Adams.

School

I went to school here at Jocko for two years. We'd leave to school about around 4:00 I guess; I don't even remember the time. We had to walk down and back to the camp. We was camped down by the river then. My folks didn't believe in it, that's why I ain't got much school. That's why I had all my kids finish school 'cause I didn't. Some folks didn' really push 'em for school, if they want to go they go, if they don' want to go they don' go. If they lived too far, 'bout two or three miles they don't go.

The first work was say my A B C's. Then after that I guess the next day, I never really took care of that, had to start countin'. We us'ta do 25, that's as far as we us'ta go. Thought we was right there then [really good]. Then we start in on our A B C's, then I guess when we got a little better we'd start spelling, cat and all that, dog. Then we'd start in our 50's countin', went to hundred, boy we sure knew what we's talkin' 'bout.

The nuns they were supposta be nice, but [they weren't always nice]. I liked it, but it's only just that they wouldn't let us talk Indian. When we'd get together that's all there was. So when we'd get together we'd all sneak away and get to talkin', but if we got caught, they sure hit you!

Sickness and Curing

The next fall they took us to St. Ignatius [1915], we had to stay there. That's when I got sick and they made me quit. I never went back. The kids, they stay there September til June, they really made us stay. I think that's why a lot of them parents didn' want to see their kids leave. Once in a while not often, parents would visit. We had no vacation like Thanksgivin' and Christmas and all that. Now they have all kinds of 'em. My mom would drop us off in September and not pick us up till June.

I was 'bout eleven when I was goin' to school in St. Ignatius, Charity Sisters. Remember them havin' them swing boards; they're like this, they go like this kinda small. We were goin' like that, somebody pushed me down. I don' know, I was sick for I don't know how many years. I spent my sick months at St. Pats [St. Patrick's Hospital in Missoula]. They couldn't help me there; they said I had TB from that.

My folks brought me home and went to the Indian doctor. He couldn't do it. I stayed home one fall, must've been this time of year [Fall]. One old man went back with my dad. I was layin' there, he says "What's the matter?" My dad says the doctors says she's got TB. This old man says "I'll get her medicine tomorrow." He was from Washington. He says you get my horse early in the mornin', just breakin' daylight. I'm goin' to this canyon over here. He says you give me a flour sack. You know that's all they us'ta have was flour sacks; you wash 'em. He says just give me one of those and I'll get her some medicine. Early in the mornin' before I was awake that guy was gone. I found he was gone when I woke up. I waited for him to come. Must be 'bout 10 or 11:00 he got back on horseback. So then he told my mother to have water, hot water. They us'ta have a kettle sittin' on the stove. Soon as he got

Agnes helps dig camas out of cooking pit at her camp in
Valley Creek.
Courtesy Séliš–Qlispé Culture Committee,
St. Ignatius, Montana

back he tell my mother he wanted one of them pots, you know
tin pots. It started boilin', boy was I in a hurry to drink, it smelled
real good. He stood there and my mother tried to tell him, you'd
better eat. He says no, when she drinks then I'll eat. He stood
there and watched the pot. He took two cups pour some in, start
goin' pourin', try to make it get cold right away. So he tasted it, a
little too hot and he poured it back and poured it back in [back
and forth between the two cups]. Now you taste it now he said,
so I take it and it was just red, a really nice color. He took it and
then he told me pray and make sign of the cross, so I did. So I
drank almost half the cup. He told me now I can eat. He told my
dad in 'bout three days she'll be up. They have to lift me up and I
coughed and coughed and lay down again. So in three days I get
up and go to the bathroom. We didn't have no bathroom in the
house, so I have to walk. My mother'd be holdin' me. I told her I
think I can make it, you don't have to help me.

So he says I'm going back to Washington. My mom gave
him a blanket. He says what's that for? My mother says I'm givin'
it to you, so he took it. So they walked to Arlee, us'ta be a train
going down [to Spokane] 4:00 in the afternoon. So they got to
the depot and my dad got him a ticket. He says what's that for?
My dad says because we're friends. He said I thought you was
payin' me. He says no, we're friends. I don't know how long then
I was back on my feet. I had pictures, I was just a skeleton.

Learning Old Ways

I jus' follow my mother. Whatever she does, that's what I'd
learn. I was lucky, had my mother then. That's how I learned all
these things, all kind of work, berries, roots and medicine.

Like quill work, I'd have to sit there by my mother. She says
now you do this. Then she flattens the quill and she puts it on.
See them quills got no needle, got no thread. It's just a quill. So
she'd tack the end, you watch it. She'd tack it over here then she
bends it, tack it over here. Then she goes so far and says now you
know what I'm doin'? I think so. She says just watch me again.
She get another quill, she puts 'em in like the other and it gets a

little bit longer. Then she goes and tacks it down goin' zigzag, you know. She makes all kind of outfit, makes buckskin and leather. Quills were the first beads, didn't have no beads, cheap beads. I like the big quills.

Somedays Vic gets a porcupine. A lot of 'em [people] pick huge ones [quills], pick one and try to pull it off. You hit it with a blanket [to get the quills in the blanket] then I go like this, pick about four of them. It's easy to pick 'em off. Just like you pull right out, pull it, cut it.

My grandma didn't bead. By that time she's gettin' old, my mother did. I just put beads on another needle, then I have my tack needle and tack it down. You can try it on anything [any kind of fabric]. There's some a little bit thicker I like. I'm makin' a vest, I got this far to go and then the back. If I just sit here and work on it, it doesn't take long.

I told 'em anybody wants to learn just do it. Doug Allard always says it's Agnes's word, do it. I say sure, do it! If you don't do it you're never gon' learn. I says that's the way my mother us'ta tell me, do it, finish it. They quit and I says do it. Take a small project not a great one. I says after you get good then you start on a big one. Some men just got started. Guess they thought it was fun watchin' their women, jus' started beadin'. Some 'em really can bead too. Like this loom work, it's a different kind of tackin', so I showed him how to bead. You take four beads and come out on two then put four again, looks like they're both tacked. This nurse she had two needles. I says just use one needle, so she like it. They have something for theirself.

We have sweat house up there [at camp]. At home down there where that little shack is, is another one. Whenever you have the time in the evenin' [you sweat]. If you have nothin' to do in the evenin', like sometimes you have to go someplace or you have something to do in the house, you forget about the sweat house. Then if you have nothin' to do, [you say] oh I'm gon' build a sweat. So that's what they been doin' [at camp]. They're sweatin' every night, I told 'em not me yet, it's a little too cold [outside in early May]. Got two sweat houses [at camp], one

here and one way over there, a big one over there. It could hold a
dozen I guess. That's the mens.

Farming

Well since I remember I was over there at Arlee. See my
dad us'ta farm all down there where they call it Indian Village
on the other sid'a Arlee, where all them houses are across the
highway. My dad started farmn' all that place into Arlee. What I
remember, like we had a house down on the other side of Arlee.
Our house was down by the river. He has one room kinda put
a partition in there and fills it with grain, 'cause they have pigs
and chickens. Then people go over there, they wanted some for
their chickens and whatever they had. He'd go and fill their sack.
Pretty soon there was a big hole where you get wheat for other
people.

We had a log house. After they, my grandma and my dad
died, and it was just my grandma and her boy and my mother and
me, they tore it down. They just tore it down, said a log house'll
get really rotten. But if somebody stay [had stayed] there, see
we were all scattered, all got married, so that's why. That's what
went bum, it really did. You can't even trace where the house us'ta
be. My grandma sold the land to the tribe. That's why all them
houses are there.

We had some pigs down where Jocko Store is, that Jocko
Store down on the river. He had a bunch of pigs there and cows
and chickens [Agnes's father]. He had chickens you know them
Bantams, them big gray ones. We had pigs they were all down in
there where Jocko store is and fenced across the road. Well there
wasn't no road there. The road us'ta be on top of that, and there
was cows and there us'ta be a bridge there. So they had nothin' to
do with cows that's where we had all our pigs. We had cows and
I don't know what to count them or not. I just seen 'em there,
don' know how many we did or didn't have then. There was all
kinds of pasture down across the river. When they get through in
the lower pasture they'd take the horses back to Valla Creek. My

dad had a place over there. There was a lot of pasture, then one day it was just gone.

My dad he just did that farm himself. He'd hire about two boys to walk and plow. Walk and plow's a pretty slow job. We'd walk and plow, didn't have no tractor then. He us'ta cover all that place, where that tepee village is. It's a land he planted and plowed. Like when my dad us'ta cut his grain you know, they us'ta bale it. Soon's he get one brother, one sister and I, and I had an auntie and a uncle. There was five of us kids together. Soon as my dad would turn his back on us, we'd go over there and go into shocks and he'd get mad at us. He says you unpile it.

We baled the hay you know. My dad says go stand it up just enough for a load. He'd go over there and see there's three loads. He says to me stand 'em up alone. He didn't like that. We were suppos'ta have 'em in bunches. We just stand 'em up as far as we could, we'd pile it just as long as we could. So they'd stop their wagon and load it on. They us'ta thrash you know. The thrashin' machine takes a lot a men to run. They take care of the straw, take care of the grain. There was just a lot of them. A guy'd be runnin' the engine feedin' it with water and wood, only that to make it run. It had a long belt, because that belt was goin', the long one to the thrashin' machine and to the motor. Then guess everybody's busy, we have to try to run through that big belt. It was jus' wide. After, later I used to think of that.

When he gets done thrashing he hauled his grain to DeMers and St. Ignatius. He us'ta go in and get this flour. He'd go in and like they'd trade, sack of wheat for a sack of flour, I don' know how it goes. He comes back with a load of flour. That makes us go through all winter. We didn't have to buy flour. In them days you didn't have to go to the store everyday, long as you got meat and flour. My dad us'ta bring his grain into Mission [St. Ignatius] and get flour. Then we'd have a big stack of flour. People would go over there and trade my mother for flour.

Even when we camped down there [by the river] my dad had nine milk cows. So the rest of the camp has to have milk. We'd have to, us kids, drive our cows back to the corral and milk.

Agnes and Jerome Vanderburg in 1959.
Courtesy Séliš–Qlispé Culture Committee,
St. Ignatius, Montana

So they's waitin', 'cause when one [person] would come with a bucket, pretty soon it's all gone. When my kids growed up I us'ta have milk cows. I tell 'em try and milk. They'd milk, just like a thread comin' out. I'd get tired 'a standin' there watchin'. I got a stool, I'd sit there with both hands, it's easy to milk, they said we can't.

See mom us'ta have this really good garden. The biggest thing we put in was potatoes and carrots and onions, lettuce, radish, stuff like corn. We had one old Indian got sick from them turnips, them white ones. We us'ta cut the top off and scratch it, makes it kinda damp for you to eat. We kept givin' him some, we gave him too much he got sick, that night he heaved. He got all right. When you scrape it it's kind of juicy and sweet, but you just take it and bite it, it don't taste too good. We always have to cut the top and we started scrapin'. She [mother] us'ta never can corn. When the corn was fresh, she braids them and hangs them up. Then later she takes a knife and cuts it off. Then she sticks 'em in sacks just like beans. I never did see her can corn.

Jerome and Agnes's Farm

When we first got married we didn't do nothin'. Jerome didn' do nothin'. Later he started plowin', grain in there and all over. This was all grain across on the other side of Lucy's. I don't know how many years then he quit. Got tired, just puts it up for hay. Like Eneas, he's out now. That's the way Jerome was, goes out, comes back for a meal, goes out workin' on the farm. He didn't hunt that much. Jus' once in a while they, some of his friends get together and go out. Go out for about three days, then they start'd workin' on these trails and had horses. See we had eight pack horses and his saddle horse, so he moves the group all over you know.

Jerome was with that guy when they appraised the reservation. He said he was seventeen so he was a help packin' lot'a stuff. When he got really old and I was tellin' him about the Jocko, I said they move our land, it's way on this side. He was kinda shakin' and he says I wish I could get there I'd show'em where the line was, the reservation line.

Allotment

I remember, but didn't know what year my parents got their land. My dad he got on the horse, saddle, and went to Agency [Jocko] and then went over there and they pick out the land where they want to live. That's how we ended up in Valla Creek. He put me there and my brother and my sisters there and him and my mother. See up on the flat it's so many acres, then if it's uphill you get 160 acres. When gets flat ground like you can farm then you get 80.

They us'ta do that [allot for new babies]. I don' know for how many years, but they quit that. It kind'a ends right there. Like anybody gets a kid they don' get, well they're enrolled but they don' get any land anymore. Well they can't anyway, it's all taken. This is all Vanderburg land. See it started over there by Finley Creek. That's where the first old man Vanderburg lived. That's why this is all Vanderburg place. They pick out where they want' to live. So sometimes kids didn' pick out theirs, so their folks did. They're the ones that's in timber. They were the ones that got a chance to get a little money off 'a their timber. Their folks didn't know that timber was gon' be good price so they put the kids [land] up high.

Hunting

Huntin', that's what his sport was [Agnes father]. Every fall we'd go way over past Seeley Lake on that pass. I don't know what they call it now, had all Indian names. Like two years ago we went through here and named every campin' ground. They all got different names, Indian names. We'd stay there 'til after Thanksgivin', pretty close to Christmas, then we'd come home. Every year I could just barely remember us goin' every year. I don't even know what month. Sometimes if he don't get done thrashin', he'd stay home and us, our bunch would go ahead of

him 'til he gets done. It's been like that since before he start on
the farm.

We'd go, my mother's got baby, it didn' bother her [to trav-
el]. They us'ta make me sit down and hold the baby while they're
puttin' the tepee up, cover me up and everything. They'd cover
the poles.

Childhood, Racing

Well, when I got to be 17, 16, I started trainin' for racing. I
won three races, 17, 18, and 19. I traveled for racing. Everytime
they're gonna be races someplace I always come up. I was small
you know, it was pretty good. When I first tried practicin' racin'
it was like the wind was goin' take my breath and my dad says
don't open your mouth when you're goin'. I got my mouth open
when we take off, so I got to learn all that, how to ride.

Then third year we'd have relay races. We have four horses.
You jump off, put your saddle on the other one, get on. One rid-
er half a mile, each horse'd go half a mile. That's the same track
we got in Missoula. If it's one mile you gotta go 'round twice.
Then if it's half a mile, you go, start over there come and stop.
Maybe that's why I can't hardly walk. Jump off, your cinch is
hooked like that with whatever it was made. You pull it all apart
and under the stomach kind'a stretches. Put it off, throw it on
your horse, reach for your cinch under your horse then hook it
again and get on and go. I always make it, I never got beat once,
even on a tepee race.

We'd have tepee race right there in Missoula. They us'ta
shoot for starter. They'd shoot, we'd start right in front of the
grandstand. See you have your horse, put some poles on the side
of the horse, then the tepee canvas was on top of the saddle. We'd
drop our poles and take the canvas off. Somebody takes our horse
away 'cause the poles are just bendin' like that, hit somebody, just
too bad. Then we'd tie three or four poles together, put it up. Put
some more poles, tie the canvas on to another pole, put it up,
cover it and pin it, chest pins. So we had paper and grass to start
our fire. So we get done [erecting their tepee]. Then my partner'd

take the paper, we was cheatin' then [by using paper]. She'd burn that paper 'cause we was inside the tepee. She stuck it so smoke gets to run right out. Then she'd drop it in the middle and we'd step all over it. We went out and the grandstand just screamed and hollered. Our partner, their tepee was upside down. That's why they were all screamin'. So we got our horse back, tied the poles back. We took the tepee then we took off, we won!

Different guys say you use my horse for racin', ok. We don't even know how the horse'll take those poles and he's got to drag them. So we tried it anyway, it worked alright. Then this old man says, "You don't have to wrap your pole in this kind of tie." He made three loops like that, way and long. I don't know whatever he did. There was a loop here, loop here and loop here. He says, "Be sure and have the other end go through and pull it, it's done." When we were goin' put the tepee up, our partner they left their tepee pole and they got to wrap it. This old man showed us the easy way. I never got to know how that works and now they're [the ones who knew this method] all gone.

We got three horses in our other pasture. I can't get up on their back anymore, I gotta have a ladder. If the horse was standin' there and wait for you, would be kind and let you get on. Them two they just go 'round and 'round while you got the reins, you're holdin' and they're too quick. Then these three others ain't broke.

Tepees

My mother gave me one tepee, I start'd goin' out. I made trips into the mountains. Then later I start' makin' my own. I used to watch my mother and one old lady make. She used to tell me come over here and watch us. So that's how I learned how to make it. We had to sew by hand, spread it out and sit on the canvas. Now I got Lucy's girl. Lucy and these two girls, they know how to make tepee.

When I used to live with my folks, we used to get the fir boughs and stick them as you want to lie down. Then you put your beddin', rugs and canvas, fix your beddin'. There was my dad and my mother and me and my sister and brother, that's five. There was always about three beds. We weren't crowded, in a big tepee you can have your head towards the wall. You can't get squeezed out. You keep it open right by the fire.

You got them earflaps, it keeps wherever the wind is comin' from, you have to work the flaps. If it comes right straight for you, you have to close it. That's what them flaps are for. Air comes in the bottom.

I made one tepee, kinda short and fat, for two people, 'bout as high as the ceiling, nine-footer. You could change the pattern. The one we had at camp was a 21-footer when I cut it. It was too big. I put the poles in, put the canvas on, kinda saggy. I got the scissors and I cut it, cut about two feet. We had 31 people in that.

Just this tribe don't do no drawin' on their tepees. I don't know why, just a plain old tepee. You'd make tepees in the summer, take a coupl'a days. I didn' make 'em out of skin; canvas. Got a call from Billings about three years ago, guy wanted buckskin tepee. I had a partner she was talkin', she says, lets take that. I says no way, we're not gon' make it. Said they'll give us $2,500. I says no, it's too hard. I made three tepees this summer [1981]. I didn't sew. I'd have Lucy, she cut it out. She's pretty good. So when I'm not here, she can do it. Marsha too, she made one all by herself. I'd just sit there and show her. I take my pedal sewin' machine up there to camp. I've made a lot of tepees with that. We sure need it, lot of them want to make tepee up there for theirselves. They bring it up there, I make 'em do it.

There us'ta be poles all over where we us'ta camp. When we were gonn' move camp, they take care of our tepee poles. Everybody comes back. They go right straight to where their poles are. Now there's hardly nobody puts their tepee up. You go, you think you got tepee poles over there, you go there and somebody chopped 'em. When you're campin' you don't need to carry them. Somebody must've burned for wood. Just use lodgepole, if you can't find that you can use tamarack, boy they're heavy. They're easy to bend and sag, but lodgepole they stay straight up.

We use four poles and about fifteen more, depends on how big your tepee is. You use more poles if your tepee is big, but fifteen for a twelve-footer. There's different tribe, like they use three [pole foundation]. Like one in front and two in back, then they lay all the extra poles on it. Around here they always would have four. See there's two over there and two in back then they start laying up the extra poles. It don't matter, you can mix 'em [the poles] together when you take your tepee down. You don't know which one is the four. Pick out any one and tie them together. But the earpole is the one that's separate. Have a skinny one for the flap. These poles are longer in the back. Then you lay your poles here, some on the other side, then you lay another one here they all come up. You have to lay 'em like this [she puts her hands together with her fingers interlocking]. Then your earpole is separate outside. It depends on how big your tepee is, nine-footer or ten-footer, can put two supporting poles on each pole but you still got'a have the four [main poles].

Eneas us'ta trap like maybe in November. They start' goin' in Jocko. They go so far and they make tepee out of so many poles. They get all kind of cedar boughs, you know they're nice and flat. They cover their poles and they fix their beddin' like that. They make hole for the door. You just stick 'em in there. See they're flat, just stick 'em in there any way. Then they make a fire and have something for their door. That's the way they go. Then they trap, I don't know for how long, they go trap mink and marten.

Courtship and Marriage

It was all very scary you know. He [Jerome] was raised back down here, a good ways from this place. He was married before. I didn't care much about him. He didn't seem to bother me much when I see him 'cause he had two kids and his wife. Then after she died he had been, got in jail. I don't know what he did.

Then we was in Missoula digging bitterroot. We us'ta catch that streetcars, take you out anywhere you want to go. There us'ta be streetcars when we was camped in Missoula. One time I got

Agnes and Jerome Vanderburg, 1960
Courtesy Lucille Otter, Ronan, Montana

in and he [Jerome] was there and after, he was goin' get off the streetcar he says "gon' take you to show." I had friend, she was from Coeur d'Alene, he had partner too. He says you both come tonight. I din' know what to say and then my partner says ya. So that evenin' we got ready and we went and met the streetcars. Got in and they came in and so they sit with us. She wanted to sit with that other guy so I sat with Jerome. After that we got to town, Missoula town, got off right in the middle of the street. Went to the show. After that, after show, we went on the street-cars. We went back to the camp. 'Bout the next day we went out came back to Missoula and eversince. Then I couldn't see him anymore. He was scared of my folks I guess. For all of summer and all August, around August he got over there. He says "I got the license, we're gonna get married." He didn' ask. So we got Mrs. Coombs and Mr. Coombs to come with us. We went to the Mission [in St. Ignatius] and got married on August 21st. My mom and dad knew. Eversince then we stayed with each other, for 53 years, the same face. That's why I always tell the kids, don't get married for just a couple of days, couple weeks, couple years, that's forever.

After we got married we stayed with my uncle [mother's brother], Ray Adams for one year. We had this house leased to Bert Eldridge. We got it back, we stayed here in this old house eversince 1921. Jerome's parents were right down here about a quarter mile. See all this place here is Vanderburgs. We stayed here [new house] for two years before he [Jerome] died.

Pregnancy and Childbirth

You aren't supposed to eat any eggs. They said 'cause the hen just lay there and lay, lay, lay [baby will be lazy]. Then you can't eat liver 'cause you'll darken up the baby. You can't eat wild chicken 'cause the baby will cry then hold their breath. Then when you're goin' out, you go out. Don't stand and look back. When you're ready to go, you go out. 'Cause if you do that you'll have a baby already backward. Then you don't use nothin' around your neck. So you don't have no bracelets, 'cause the babies hold

Lucy and Agnes Vanderburg
Courtesy Séliš–Qlispé Culture Committee,
St. Ignatius, Montana

their breath when they're born. That's how I did it. I told my kids too, just these couple things. You can take a sweat bath and a bath in cold water.

If you just mind what you're told to eat you won't have no trouble. But right now from the start these womens eat eggs and they wish for something like liver, well they eat it. That's something like they shouldn't eat, but they want to get it so they get it. And after it's over when baby comes they don't think about the liver and all that stuff, goin' out and back in, never go out. Whatever it is they just hav'ta do that, like stop at the door, see what, there's nothin' you could see outside. Then you go back in. My grandma says get out'a here, right out!

The old timers they know what you're getting jus' by lookin' at your stomach, like now we don't even look. We see somebody big we don't even know what's comin' [which sex]. I don't know how they know, but they sure us'ta know.

What my folks us'ta tell us, when you see someone in a book or anything, like people that's crippled or in a book it's ugly. Says don't you ever watch that kind of stuff. You see one person all crippled up, don' watch it, just turn away. It will make you kind of scared. You see this crippled person or in a book, your baby'd come like that, just when you was start packin 'em. So that's the way lot of 'em have their babies all different you know. I seen it on TV, some got no arms. That's jus' how it comes, from seeing something from TV or books or they seen somebody.

After the baby comes my grandma tells us not to get up and walk. I guess you don't get out of bed. She us'ta tell us, you lay there for about two or three days. You stay there. When you want to get up you ask somebody to help you. You don' just support yourself. About oh maybe eight days you're strong enough to get up. You get up by yourself and then don't wear something that you're gonna choke, just don't do that. Then just take it easy. After that then you can get up.

My grandma she was the kind of person that did come and deliver the baby. Whatever she had [going on] she goes always, [they] have her to go. She took care of a lot of babies. No matter how late at night, no matter how late in the evenin', anytime she go. She takes care of the whole thing, 'til the womens alright. Then she'd leave. She couldn't go right in the middle of her job. She has to wait there 'til everthing's ok. So she us'ta take me along with her. She just told me how to do it, she'd do it at the job. She told me she said, "I'm gonna give you my medicine." I didn't want it. Maybe I could, but I haven't got the medicine. Just take 'em to the hospital, to the doctor. Everybody goes to the hospital now days. I just took care of my sister once. My grandma says a lot of 'em want to pay her, she says, "No, I'm working my steps up here [points to heaven]." She says maybe I'd get paid for that, I'm not workin' for pay. That's why a lot of 'em they us'ta get her, 'cause they knowed they wasn't gon' pay her. Guess everybody's cheap.

I had two babies here and two over at my mom's. It was kind'a hard. I had my grandmother to help. She died after I got Lucy. Jerome us'ta take care of the babies, he was married before. Wasn't even thinkin', thinkin' 'bout havin' a baby after you got married. After you find out you're like that [pregnant] it's too late.

I and Jerome went fishin' over Jocko. It didn't bother me when I was big you know. A lot of them I see, some of these womens can't hardly walk and can't stoop down. I knew we'd got on the horses and went fishin'. Well I don't fish I just went with him. They got back over here, we had a little log house over there. That was [when I made] my mistake, I put my leg over and I jumped. When I jump off the horse that's when I lost the baby. That evenin' I started feelin' [pain]. I didn' know what was wrong with me, it was my first one. So his mom [Jerome's] came over and said "when is it supposed to be born?" I didn't know either. So she said "you must've hurt yourself." I said no we just went fishin', got back and Jerome says "she jumped off." It didn't bother me you know. That's how I lost the one. After [that], I'd know what to do then. I had to get down slow, I don't jump off.

That's why I always tell my two girls when they start packin' their's [babies]. You musn't think your're sick. If you jus' lay around and do nothin' your baby's gonn' get just big. Move around and do something. Go on outside and do something. I didn' remember a lot of 'em [women] losing babies, just when they're sick.

Weaning Babies

As soon as they start movin' their hand, you know goin' for their mouth we give 'em some piece of hard meat, so they can work their teeth. They start eatin', suckin' on something hard. Then from now on you start feedin' 'em by little, not as much as you eat you know, just a couple a spoonfulls of something. The next day or two days you give 'em a little bit more. But the only bad thing my mother us'ta tell me when "you start feedin' your baby food, their poo's just stink." So that's why we don't hardly feed 'em right away, just when they start gettin' their teeth. If you have rice or mush or potatoes [for food] just so you know it's soft, give 'em a couple spoons. Then you don't give 'em coffee, you give 'em tea, start makin' 'em how to drink on a cup, not a bottle. I raised only one with a bottle, Lucy. Had to get up late [it was lots of bother].

Children, Jerome and Agnes

The kids, I just let 'em loose. They take care a' theirselves. Didn' hav'ta find some babysitter, you jus' do it yourself 'til they're old enough to go to school. They go to school. They'd play outside most of the time. In winter they stay in the house, but some of them they like to be outside in the winter, on their sleigh or whatever. They played everything like sleigh, just anything they could find. Then when it's really cold they stay in and have something to do in the house.

I didn't sew that much for the kids. DeMers [Mercantile] had everything we needed. They had rubbers and shoes and pants, mostly coveralls. You know them overalls that's what I had on my oldest boy. Now they're back in that style. There's a lot a pockets too.

We had cloth diapers, we didn't have these Pampers like now. We had to have regular diapers then wash it hang it out everyday. That's what the old timer used, now they have it easy. We us'ta buy lot'a cloth from DeMers, you know they had that mercantile. Don' matter what color or if it's a boy it's blue or it's a girl it's white or pink. We had all kinds of colors [of diapers]. We'd buy the cloth and cut 'em, what shape you want and what size, bigger size. Us'ta be cheap and now they want a fortune for their diapers and they're not as good.

Jerome and I used to go to the Jumping Dance. They don' have it anymore. Like the War Dance we don' go, we just wait for the fourth of July powwow. Womens don' [didn't used to] drum, but now the womens and everybody drum, dance and sing. They had that Round Dance, that's where all the womens danced, but now they're mixed men and womens dancin'. We us'ta never have that.

They never us'ta have that Camas Dance. They just started, I don't know who started that. Now there's all kind of ceremonies, like for the bitterroot. They have [had] a feast, but they don' dance. Some old timers they cooked the bitterroot. Not everybody goes, just certain ones. They have [had] that feast for the bitterroot, that's all. Now they're havin' ceremony for everything.

No, I didn't go hunting and fishing with Jerome. I us'ta tag along, after all the kids got big and then we'd go. It's not too long since we been. Our last, youngest boy takes me around. I never did go 'round with Jerome that much. But he'd go up about two or three days horseback, but before that we didn't. Just when I was with my folks we'd go. Even pickin' berries, I didn't care for that.

Older People, Visiting

They're busy like me, sittin' 'round got a lot'a stuff to do, sewing, a lot of things to do. The men they're out rustlin' wood, choppin' and haulin' it. Pass the time in the evenin', they're always busy.

Somedays we us'ta go vistin', like in the evenin' after you have your dinner. Got neighbors'd get on their horse or walk over. See in winter it's kind'a long night so "lets go visit," name the place. Us'ta go there, get over there they kept talkin' and talkin', pretty soon they start in on their story, like life, or regular stories. Sometimes it's a long story. They cut their story, "well next time you guys come here" [they will finish it]. Sometimes they're some short ones you know like 20 minutes, half an hour. It's like that you know. They sit there and talk about alot of things. Goes on and then story comes, coyote story. That's how they passed their days. See we didn't have no radio, no TV, nothin'. Jus' have the old folks sit there and tell us stories and we all got sleepy, like was their TV and radio.

Like now nobody visits. I don't know what they mean, they're too busy. Everything's different, I don't know. I don't know if they just don't like to go or if they're just lazy. I ain't got no one story in here [her head]. I jus' didn't take care of them. I always taught my kids, old people are too pitiful. They're jus' like they turn into a kid. They can't do nothin'. Somebody has to take care of them.

I says like if they could just do like we used to, the old people. They believed in everything. They don't believe in nothin' anymore.

Old Ways

They always say you ask Agnes anything, she's bound to tease us. We know her, she don't mean it. I says maybe I do! Like when they ask me something, "What was this?" I says well I wasn't takin' care of nothin', it's true [trying to remember old ways]. Like now all everybody in their twenties and thirties, they don't. There's a lot of stuff you can take care of. Like what I see now. There's a lot 'a things nobody takes care now. They want to buy everything. I was too young to keep track, it wasn't my business. What comes to me I just do it, that's all. I didn't take care of it. Like when I go to St. Ignatius they ask me a lot of questions. I says if I know then in my young days I'd keep track of everything. It goes in my one ear and comes out this other one.

It's comin' back just like I think a lot. Once in a while I'd be home, I'd think of yea, I'm gonna tell Clarence [Woodcock of the Cultural Commission] this and that. That's the way you get lot'a stories from me. I told a lot of 'em like Bearhead [Swaney]. I says whatever I tell you, it's not a lie, nobody tol' me to say this. I just know, just like I remember and woke up from a long sleep, I just woke up and thought about this. I'm gon' tell them. I says and it's true! You get old like me and then you know what to do. It's kind of late though.

That's what a lot of them want to do now [genealogies]. They should go back to start, whatever they remember 'til now. See after a lot of these old people are gone they won't find out. It's what I told Clarence. Just while you got a chance, go through how far the relation goes.

Some of 'em [kids] I guess listen to the old timers. There isn't very many old people any more. See once in a while we get together in St. Ignatius and tell 'em about what we know. I says when I talk, or on TV, they should have me talk, tell 'em 'bout what should be done. Now I'm talkin' there's just a crowd at the center in Mission. They had it dark and just where I was, there was light. I says like now there's somebody out there sayin' "Oh Agnes is talkin' for nothin'." I says I can feel it. There's jus' some of them they don't really listen. I says those that don' care to listen don' have to come and listen, but I want to say what I want to say.

A lot of my tribe they try to be white people, but they can't. They got their color. They're gon' keep their color til they're gone. I said they can't even speak their own Indian language. Like a lot of women's men they want, got the long hair. They can't make it [as an Indian]. They have to talk Indian before the can make it. Make it look like a Indian, not just because they have long hair. Some of the kids they don't care. They want to be more like white. I says no matter what you do, try and mock the white people, but there's no way you can turn into be white. You were born Indian, you're goin' be Indian all your life. That's what I told them. That's the way I feel about this.

I always tell them when I growed up I never did get drunk. I always try to be the way I am today and I says I have fun just as good as anybody that gets drunk. They say "I'm havin' fun!" I don't think that's true. I says I see a lot of people when they drink they look ugly. No matter what they do, then after they're sober, boy! You can't touch 'em with a 15 foot pole. They're so stuck up. I says I don't want you kids to ever do that. I say it's dirty what they're doin', drinkin'. I says I can put my head up and walk around, just for one reason, 'cause I never did get drunk. So they always say, "Good for you, yaya," [grandmother].

About Religion

There were two brothers, one believe and one don't. One just thought he was too pretty for somebody to push around. So this other one prays for help. So one day this other boy got sick, the one who don't pray. Guess he was Catholic, but don't believe in church and he don't talk, got no friends. He told his brother "I'm sorry, at least you were able to believe [in] somebody, I didn't." He says, "When I'm gone I'm gon'na be lost, but when you [die], you're gon' go right straight up." He says, "'Cause I don't talk to people." He was proud of himself 'cause he thought he was too pretty to believe in anybody. He says, "But you, you're always makin' the sign of the cross, that's gonna take you up there" [heaven]. He says, "It won't be too long, I'm leavin' and I'm gonna be lost." That's why everybody believe and got strong. The two brothers brought it up, it's been quite a while. We [the Flathead] were still in Stevensville.

They [the church] try and keep it back the old ways all the time. They have mass and later they have food. Like every Christmas and Easter they have that.

You can pray in the Indian way or in white, 'cause you know both of them. It's up to you. Whatever comes into your head. You don't have to be in a crowd, just be yourself.

Medicine

'Bout medicine, this guy came over. His wife she was in bed early this summer [1981] when I was campin'. He said doctor told her she had six weeks and she'd be gone. She's got cancer inside. I told him, not the way she is still alive. I says get some medicine give it to her. Then yesterday he said she's walkin' around tryin' to do something in the house. He says, "But I can't find any more of that medicine." I told her I had some. I have some in the freezer. The Indian name for it is bear ears. You make a tea whenever she wants water, she could drink it. You can't give the medicine to the person who's sick. You give it to somebody else and they'll fix it for them. It's just like a doctor.

Cradleboards

I don't know what happened to them old cradleboards, from my grandma. You know they jus' chop it by hand. My grandma jus' use a knife. She really took care of it. I don' know what happened. We should'a take care of it, we didn't. I had it when I think Annie. I don't know what happened to them old ones.

Got one of them plyboards, mark it and Vic cut it out, it's done! I made one of them papoose boards when her [Lynn Vanderburg] baby came, I gave it to her. Oh she was happy. She put her baby in there. Said she seen some of them, looks like it takes care of the baby real good. Instead of pickin' it up and it's soft. That baby likes that board. She [the baby] growed out of it. When she puts her in there's about this much stickin' out. I told her to cut it in the back, then she can be in it somemore [longer] cover herself more. We call it a sleepin' bag. It's laced through. Put some pad on the back any kind of blanket. Put your baby in and it's easy to pack.

Pneumonia and Surgery

One time I went to St. Ignatius. I had kind of pneumonia I guess. They took me. I didn' want to stay. I didn' like that hospital. The next day they [her children] picked me up. Went to my doctor in Missoula, Dr. Brooks. He told me, "You go across to Community Hospital." He says, "You go over there and I'll be over to take care of you." They brought me over there. Here in Mission [St. Ignatius] they said you pert' near got pneumonia, in Missoula they said, you got pneumonia! I thought he'd just check on me and I'd come back [home]. I stayed there five days and he says, "You go home and take care of yourself." Then I showed him my pills, sleepin' pills and all kinds of pills. He says, "Agnes you get back and throw every one of 'em away." He said, "I don't want you to use them." The doctor in Mission told me to take them. Then another time he said, "I thought you had hospital and doctor over in St. Ignatius." I told him, you want me to die [by going to that hospital and doctor]?

Dr. Brooks was my doctor for over thirty years. He operated on me, he said he couldn't put me to sleep. He said, "You got weak heart, I won't put you to sleep." That's fine with me, whatever you're gon' do with me, that's fine. He said, "I'll give you a shot, a spinal shot." I didn't feel it [the surgery].

I don't know for how many years, he said, "Agnes you're doin' fine." See I have to see him before I come up to camp and when I get back down I go to see him. Says, "All your x-rays are the same, you're ok now." He tried to get me to quit smoking. I says, "One thing I want you to do Agnes, is quit smoking." Oh I says, I can't. He says ok. I been smokin' 'bout 29 years. Jerome was sittin' there smokin', it looked good, you know, doin' it. I told him let's see your cigarette. He gave it to me, I smoked it. I told him light me another one, a strong one, Luckys. Eversince then I been smokin'. When Vic was in the service, Christmas time he sent us each three cartons of German-made cigarettes. Ok with me, we smoked it all.

Pageants and Trips

I went with Bert Hansen. I and [Carling] Malouf and all the Indians. It must be, oh, 'bout how many years they put on that pageant. That's how long I was there. One time all the Indians got real mad and they were gonn' leave because he [Bert] said,

Agnes Vanderburg
Courtesy Séliš–Qlispé Culture Committee,
St. Ignatius, Montana

"Get them to do this and get them to do that." Malouf kept saying, "Now you just have to do this and don't leave, don't leave." Everybody was gettin' real mad. They almost left and walked out on the whole thing. It wouldn't have been a very good pageant if everybody would've left.

Bert was kind'a mean. We had the tepee over here at the old agency. Mrs. Morgan she was gettin' dressed in her outfit and Bert Hansen took a blanket and he started walkin' towards the door. He grab that loud speaker and he just throw it, just missed Mrs. Morgan's face and boy she grabbed it and hollered at him, Bert.

We have five tepees put up. There was just the people over there thick. So we prayed too. We came out there and they danced in the open, Snake Dance. We us'ta go all over, wherever [they had pageants] we went, different Indians come from Dixon. Bert and Malouf could use all those Indians. They'd go over there and set the date. That's how they'd get all these Indians together. We had our last one [pageant] at the old agency, probably around the last part of May I think. That's the last pageant we had, when Bert was still alive.

Sure did travel. One time I was comin' from wherever I went, all different places, not just pageant. I was even in New York for a whole month. Did a show everday. People just from here. We went on the train. They brought the cars down in Arlee. Then they loaded up our stuff and our horses. The Indians had another car [to ride in]. We used to parade on that east side [of New York] and they'd have rodeos right inside. That was in the thirties, it was fifty-five years ago.

Las Vegas Trip

I left here at ten after 6:00. Marsha brought me over there [up to the highway] in the car. One of them people sittin' in the bus says yeah that's her [Agnes's] road right here so the bus stopped. I come on he came off took my suitcase. I went in, gee, nothin' but faces [bus was crowded]. Thirty-seven of us on Greyhound bus. So we went, it was good. He didn't have to stop

the bus for bathroom, we had the bathroom right on there. All
of them womens that know where to go [road to Las Vegas] said,
"We want to go through Salmon." But the bus driver didn't really
want to go [that way]. So he took these roads. Boy when we get
past Medicine Tree, a little ways from there it started to snow,
before we got to the pass.

When we first pulled in, in the evenin' we started eatin'
'cause there was a restaurant right there. We started eatin', I told
the bunch, "I didn't come here to eat." "I come to see what's in
there." It was just people like ants. So I seen this big jackpot
$100. I took $10. I got it all in silver. I guess some of 'em followed me, so I put $3 in and pull that handle. Boy I could jus'
hear that thing, just like fire sirens, ooooh ooooh. I thought I
broke that machine. One guy came around with an apron said,
"You got the jackpot it's $100." So he got a big kind'a paper
pocket thing was just full. I said I don't want it, it's too heavy
[coin rolls]. So he reached in his pocket gave me hundred dollar
bill. I just threw it in my purse, wide open. I left, I got all that
money in there. I carried it around, I went around. I seen there
was another place to put the quarter so I turned around and I got
[had] $8, no $7 of silver yet. I give her $2, I said give me quarters.
So she gave me quarters. Put another one in there, there it goes.
After when I hit the first jackpot I had to stop. You hit it, after
that you want to listen 'cause it's just noisy in there, you know,
everybody in there. I forgot how many times it hit it. Then when
I hit it again he says, "You hit it, $25 jackpot, you sign." I had
to sign, he gave me the money. It was all in little packages [rolls].
So he gave me $5, $10, $15. I went to start. I thought well I got
all that money in here. I went around those dime machines. I
pulled 40¢ and there it goes again. This guy came around again.
He says, "You hit it again." I said I did? I said I thought I broke
all the machines, every time I came in. Then my bunch come
around behind me and said, "Agnes you hit it again?" I said yes I
made $20. So he just give up, I just kept tellin' him I don't want
no silver, it's too heavy. He gave me $20 and I dropped it in there
[purse] and went around.

Oh there's nickels. I went back, got a bunch of nickels. Went over there, sit there sit there oh I get around eight they're all in the pot. I had another bag. I put all the nickels in there. Changed to another machine. So I got tired of those nickels I pulled a stool and sit there. I put three nickels in and pull about three times and there it comes again. Hit five times. Yeah and then this guy came around and said, "You done it again Agnes," 'cause he knew all the money was there. But that pot under all the machines is big, $43. I wanted the big big hit. He said, "What are you gon' do?" I said just for that I'm gonna take it home and show it to the kids. He went and got me one of those pockets. So I brought it back. My purse was, I set it in the suitcase, it was just heavy. So I sit there again go to another one. I didn't hit it anymore. I told my partner I'm goin' back to the room, our room was not that far. We stayed in the one [hotel] they call it Jackpot. My purse was just heavy. I went there and I set it under our bed. It was too heavy. I got all my bills and put them in my wallet and went back over there. All them guys was eatin'. I said you guys didn't come to eat. So I done pretty good.

Portland

'Bout a month ago I got on the airplane and went to Portland. There was people from all over there, different tribes. I was listenin' to them, seems like they didn' know what they were talkin' about. That guy [leader] told them, "Say something good about your reservation." They talk about cars, I didn't even like it. So they went this way [around a circle] and they got to me. I started talkin', 'bout 15 minutes. I had my arm, watchin' like this [her watch]. I didn' wan' talk too long. So I talked, everybody got up, that's the kinda word we want. Just like this guy told us, "I didn't want another one" [to talk the way they had been talking]. It's gon' be on TV. Talked about the reservation, how it is now and how folks remember it. It's pretty. You can see lot of trees. Even people are different. I'm the only one who talked like this, about our timber and water. Oh, what get in my head that's what [I talked about] so I kept goin'. I wasn' gon' quit. When them other bunch get up where they were, talked on about their wages, some Indians got no job. Well that's all over I thought when I was listening to them. I thought well everybody knows.

Then my partner, my brother's boy, everything was quiet, he say, "Well what auntie [Agnes] said." He was facin' them. He says oh, he started talkin' 'bout sweat house and on, got to grizzly bear. Says, "In our reservation we got the grizzly bear and we try and protect them." I told him, protect them?, I says no shoot 'em! We want to get rid of them. There's a lot of campin' around and everybody's scared. I says shoot 'em. Everybody smiled. There used to be a lot of them wolves, but you don't hardly hear them. You don't see them too.

Agnes demonstrates her independence constantly by traveling on and off the reservation, participation as a speaker in numerous programs and conferences and her camp in the mountains. Agnes's camp also demonstrates her desire to be "with nature." She explained how she prays before gathering plants because,

You have to tell 'em what you're goin' do. You have to pray, 'cause it's what I hear my grandmother say Bitteroot's got a heart, they say a heart. It's a seed I guess you could call it. So if you don't take care of it right, they go back in the ground. You won't find nothin'. I says, when people believe, it's ok. I says I want to show you kids, young people now what we went through and everything was ok, berries and roots, really we had a lot of 'em to take care of for the winter. Sometimes in the summer you don't hardly get certain kind of berries. I says you know why? One little berry gets ripe and you run for it and grab it and eat it. You don't even wait for somebody to tell you do this and eat it. That's why we're losin' all our berries [greed]. A lot'a you don' care, bunch of people don't believe in what we're tryin' to show should be done. Anything, you have to pray for it, no matter what, berries, [etc.]. Them wild strawberries'll be next. Take two and be sure and think about 'em, don't just say oh Agnes is talkin' for nothin'.

Agnes went on speaking about the past matter of factly and spoke on the subject of health as so many of the Native American women had. This is Agnes's recollection about past health conditions.

Long time ago, when I just kinda knowed people, when I was little, too young, I was wide awake and that's all. I was just a live person that didn't know what was going on. They had that one sickness, Chickenpox or smallpox? Smallpox, they come out like bumps. If you don't take care of it, they [the bumps] go back in and that's when they die. But you have to take care of them and they can stay out. When they get dry they're like dry scab and that means you're well. That's the time I seen those. One day they were buryin' two people. I remember really good about them, two old ones, a man and a woman. That must've been really bad that time, that's the only kind I know [illness] they just die. I don't even know how many days they were sick. My folks said that's the kind they had. My dad says they shut Evaro, that's as far as you could go, Evaro. Nobody couldn't go through Evaro to go to Missoula. Then from there they couldn't come in the reservation, 'cause on a count'a that sickness. Must'a be really bad. [The reservation had a severe smallpox epidemic in 1901.]

Agnes then went on to explain her assessment of current health states, and mentioned specifically cancer and heart disease as recent ailments among her people.

In my time we don't see people have arthritis. You know their fingers are all bent and their hands. What is it? Is it what they eat or what they drink, what is it? Them old ladies they shrunk so small and they'd get around just really good. Jus' like they're 'bout 30 or 40. They could get on their horses and go. But now the car, they walk to the car, they don' have't walk no more. So that's what the difference is to me. I can't understand these two sicknesses, heart attack and cancer. Every time I see it on TV or anything cancer, cancer. This heart attack is what I can't figure out, and cancer. There's sure a lot'a cancer, kill a lot'a people. What is it?

Agnes spoke little about the comparison of present and past. When she did comment, most often there was no stated preference for the way of one time period over another. However, she did make . . . statements about what she felt is different now than when she was younger.

There's a lot'a things I always tell my kids, you should'a seen it when I was young. It is different in a way [now]. Like what's different to these kids of mine now. It's all this electricity and cars, that's the difference from what I went through. Like food, that's different now too. I was raised on wild game and fish and birds and now they want everything tame. That's the difference to me I always tell 'em. In a way some things are better [now]. Like the kids now they missed what I had, horses and buggies and sleighs and what we us'ta have, but now they got this snowmobiles, bikes and motorbikes.

Source: Barbara Springer Beck, "Agnes Vanderburg: A Woman's Life in the Flathead Culture," unpublished master's thesis, University of Montana, Missoula, 1982, pages 51-87 and 92-95.

A Visit with Agnes

Interview by Thompson Smith and MQTV

July 1986

Tom: What we're doing with this videotape project is to try to find out how things have changed on the reservation since the [Flathead Lake] dam was built. It doesn't necessarily have to be stories about the dam itself, although it could be. But anything that you think has been a really big change since that dam went in. Do you remember when the dam was being built? How old were you at that time?

Agnes: I must be in my fifties, forty or fifty.

Tom: In what ways do you think the reservation was different at that time?

Agnes: The story I look at it, it was sure different. When I growed up it was really good.

Tom: How so? How was it better than now?

Agnes: Well, like you try have a horse, you can't leave your own place. Too many fences, too many gates. Every place you go there is no trespassing. You can't ride all day, unless you really want to go through somebody's property and get in trouble. When I growed up there was hardly no fence.

Tom: Now there is a lot more private property signs right.

Agnes: Everybody's got their ten acres, five or ten acres on up. Got it fenced.

Tom: Back then was there more land that was owned by the tribe as a whole?

Agnes: Yea, the whole thing was nothing but tribe land. To me it was just like it was free for Indians to go around. But now you can't. You have to be on the highway before you are free.

Tom: So that's one of the big changes that has occurred in your mind.

Agnes: Yea.

Tom: You would have been about ten years old when the reservation was opened to whites. Right?

Agnes: Yea. It was about 1910 or 1912. That when all the Indians had their own land. They pick out which place they want. That's how it happened.

Tom: How was it before that?

Agnes: What do you mean?

Tom: The land wasn't owned before that? People could just go anywhere before that.

Agnes: You just go anyplace. There was no fence. Just little dirt road for a wagon. It's not paved.

Tom: So, they called that allotment, right, when they divided it up. Were there Indians who tried to stop that from happening?

Agnes: That's something I don't know about.

Tom: So, you remember that time when the reservation was opened to whites. Did they just come in all of sudden one day?

Agnes: No, there was only one guy I know. There was a meeting, and he said, "Anybody wants to get their patent. Come and sign right in front of me, and then you can sell your land to white people." That's when they done something wrong. A lot of them was starting lining up and signing up. That's how a lot of these Indian lands were sold to white people.

Tom: And shortly after they opened the reservation, they started the irrigation project up. Is that right?

Agnes: Yea, they have a little meeting just the old timers, no women, no kids. They go in one house and talk about what a person was told that there was going to put a ditch in Jocko. Some didn't understand. Why they thought they were going to dry the river. They said no. Before they dig the water there was a lot of them used to put a garden, a little crop, oats, wheat, barley. But after they got settled down, all the Indians moved up Jocko. They all had teams, walking plow. They all work with the Reclamation outfit. They had mules for their team. So, after that they went clean to Jocko store. That's where it ends. And on the other side of the river they went as far as Bob Schall's. That's where that ditch ends.

Tom: So, the Indians thought that it was alright since they would be getting water for their gardens?

Agnes: I didn't know what was what. First thing I know, folks say we got a water bill. So, they tried to fight them again, but they couldn't make it. Cause they said they were going to get free water after they run all these streams coming into the ditch. Some they have their own water rights. Like we got there. That belongs to my kids. We got a record for that.

Tom: So, did a lot of Indians grow their own food at that time? Gardens?

Agnes: That's how they do. They have all kinds of garden stuff.

Tom: So, with the opening of the reservation and the irrigation project and then the land getting fenced off and changed to private property, that must have changed the whole way of life people had in a lot of ways.

Agnes: In a way you can see who sold their land. They were the first ones that had a car, cut their hair, had a collar — that stiff collar they called it. You could easily tell which one took the patent. Some just stayed in Arlee. There was a hotel there. They stayed right there. They spent their money right there.

Tom: Did they seem proud to have those new things?

Agnes: They sure did.

Tom: And were there others who were proud not to have those things?

Agnes: Some said, "When you go broke I don't want you ever come to my door and beg. You want to put your tepee or something you got on my land." They were told, but still a lot of them took it, anyway.

Tom: That's very interesting.

Agnes: Yea.

Agnes Vanderburg
Courtesy Lucille Otter, Ronan, Montana

Tom: And you said that a lot of Indians when the irrigation project came in, they didn't quite understand what was happening. Why do you think they didn't understand?

Agnes: I believe they didn't, cause their interpreter, there's a lot of words they translate. You can't do it. I know this old man, he didn't really talk really good Indian. He's the one that says okay or just alright. So, that's how it went. They didn't understand each other.

Tom: So, whites ended up being able to get the Indians to agree to things that if they had known about it, they wouldn't have agreed to it?

Agnes: There was one old man, when they surveyed where they were going to put their ditches in, they have little sticks, you know, marking their ground. When they're all gone, this old man goes through there with a gunny sack. He pulled every one of them. And he goes to the river and burned all them little stakes. He didn't want no ditches to go through. Right there were the powwow ground is.

Tom: Who was that?

Agnes: Sam Resurrection. He tried his best, but he was all alone. Nobody couldn't help him. Couldn't talk for him.

Tom: Why didn't other Indians join with him?

Agnes: I don't know. They just didn't care to join him. He was the one that run around for that settlement from Stevensville. He's the one that got it. If it wasn't for him, we would never have got it.

Tom: He went to Washington.

Agnes: Yes, he goes to Washington. He tries to go around, get some money from everybody, so he would have some money to go in. So, he get on freight, hitchhike, whatever he could do. He finally got in to Washington.

Tom: Why was his name Sam Resurrection? How did he get that name?

Agnes: Cause, he died when he was about three or four years old. His little legging was all wore. His moccasins was poor. So, his mother and another woman was making a new pair for him while he was laying there dead. After they was just about done with everything, this other old lady said, "Look at your boy." She looks, and, "My boy ghosted me?" She went over there and picked him up. "Why, you are alive?" He says, "No, I was sleeping."

Tom: Where was he? Was he lying in a coffin?

Agnes: No, there was no having a coffin at the time. That was still in Stevensville when it happened. So, that's how they called him Resurrection. They tried to ask him what he seen. And he said "No." He thought he was sleeping.

Tom: I heard that ever after that he would always go to people's wakes. He really made it a point to go to all those.

Agnes: Yea, he never missed one wake. No matter how far he'd walked over there.

Tom: Was he still alive the time Jerome died?

Agnes: No, he died before Jerome did.

Tom: Did Jerome know him well?

Agnes: Yea. My oldest boy got to know him.

Tom: Eneas.

Agnes: But the rest of them didn't.

Tom: There's some other things I was wondering about. The dam and the changes that came since them. Did you know a lot of people who worked on the dam when it was being built?

Agnes: Those ones that I remember. Those died, some didn't. There's Tony Adams, he died. Paul Eneme. Agnes Kenmille's husband. And....

Tom: Did Jerome work on the dam?

Agnes: No.

Tom: Why not?

Agnes: I don't know. They didn't.

Tom: He could've if he wanted to?

Agnes: Yea. I think he had a crop. He had a crop here. Just his boy went, but he didn't. He made it through. Baptiste Sapia and then that Mexican, what you call, Hernandez. Heard a lot of them worked there. They all made it.

Tom: A lot of people worked there. It was mainly because people needed the jobs, right? That's what a lot of people who worked there told me. The reason everybody went there to work was because they were pretty poor at that time. Compared to now, in what ways were most people a lot more poor at that time?

Agnes: Well, I don't know how. There was just no jobs for them, you know. So, that's the way I see it. There were just no jobs. If there were jobs a lot of them goes. Like when that CC camp started at Jocko. Jerome put in three years up there. They were getting only $1.10 a day. And then the food was cheap too. So, we got along with just even that much. They don't get paid in two weeks, they get paid once a month.

Tom: What kind of things did people have to buy in a store at that time?

Agnes: Like flour and sugar and coffee, and things like that. That's the main.

Tom: Kerosene?

Agnes: Yea.

Tom: So, a few basics people could get in the store. I remember you once told me that for a long time, until maybe the 1930s, a lot of people would go in the Bitterroot in the summertime to pick berries and fruit. Did you do that?

Agnes: A lot of them [unintelligible]. They don't go over there to get a little half a pound, two pound. The get them in these sacks. Just fill it up. That makes for a whole winter's food of bitterroot. And then when sarvis berries comes that's what they do too. They dry it. It's not just a little bucket full, another sack full. Huckleberries, choke cherries. They's always getting ready for the winter. And when fall comes, everybody goes in a different direction going hunting.

Tom: Did your family do that?

Agnes: We used to go to the other side of Seeley Lake. And then Jerome's folks go to Fish Creek.

Tom: Where did you go after you got married?

Agnes: The same place.

Tom: Over by Seeley?

Agnes: Yea.

Tom: So, Jerome would go where your family went.

Agnes: Yea.

Tom: How long would people go hunting for?

Agnes: Well, until they figured they had enough for the winter. They dried. Everything was got to be dried. There was no refrigerator, no deep freeze to put it away. So, everything's dried.

Tom: So, when did that stop happening? When did people stop going off in the fall hunting and picking berries in the summer?

Agnes: Well, it's the jobs now. Lot of them is working now. The man's working. The woman's working. So, it's all different now. Since they got a car, they don't care to go up any more.

Tom: What do you think's going to happen when the gas runs out and there are no more cars?

Agnes: Go back the same way.

Tom: If you want to, tell the story you told me up there at your camp about when you were healed when you were a little girl. When you were sick.

Agnes: I went to school. I must have been around nine. I went to school over here at Jocko for two years. And went to St. Ignatius charities for two years. Then I got sick. Kids pushed me off from their swing. I don't know what you call that. It was just boards.

Just barely moving. They pushed me off from there, and ended up in hospital. I don't know for how long, and my dad came after me. He says, "I am going to take you back and bring you to Missoula hospital." So, St. Pat's was still small. That's where I went. I stayed in there for about six months. My dad went over there and, "We can't do nothing about that, she's got TB." So, I came back. He says, "I will take you to Indian doctor." So, he took me to Indian doctor. I couldn't do nothing. Next, he took me to Valley Creek. He was supposed to be a smart doctor, medicine man. Couldn't do nothing. So, he brought me home. [uninteligible] something I didn't know nothing about. I was lying in bed.

One evening my dad walked in. He had a partner. I didn't know him. Kind of an old man. He stopped right by my bed. He said, "You have a sick daughter, uh?" My dad said, "Yea, she's got TB." He said, "I'll fix her. She'll be alright." So, he turned around and told my mom, "Tomorrow you get me a flour sack." Cause flour sack, they used to take care of flour sack, sugar sack. It's got to be white, clean. Told my nephew, "Get my horse," before daylight. First, I am going up in the hills and get some medicine for her. The next morning, I woke up. I told my mother, "Where is he?" Said, "He's gone already." And I waited and waited. Told my mother to have a lot of hot water, really hot. Because we had the wood stove, kettle there.

One of my sisters had a brother, said "There he comes." Boy I was glad to hear it, he has come. He got back. My dad went out and took care of the horse. Brought him to the barn. Came in. My mother said, "Oh, everything is ready." He said, "I want one pot. It must be galvan[ized] pot, not aluminum, not tin." So, she said she's got one. So, he turned his back from me. I didn't know. I was really watching, but I couldn't see when he started putting the medicine in the pot. He opened that lid and put that pot there. I don't know how long I could smell that medicine boiling. Gee, I sure wish I was drinking already, because I was sick for quite a while. So, he stood there. My mother told him, "Ain't you going to eat breakfast." "Wait until Agnes gets done with her medicine, and then she is going to eat, and I'll eat." So,

Agnes Vanderburg
Courtesy Séliš–Qlispé Culture Committee,
St. Ignatius, Montana

he took the pot away. Got two cups. One empty one. He filled one. He kept pouring this empty one back and forth. So, he tried it so it was cool enough for me. He walked up to me and says, "Now sit down." So, my mother helped me to sit down. So, I drank that medicine, a cup full. So, I'm sure feeling good. So, he told my mother, "Well, if we're going to go eat, both of us." So, she did. I couldn't. Our toilet used to be outside. I wanted to go every day. She pack me in. I couldn't be in the house. So, three days I couldn't get up and go by myself.

So, he said, "Well, I'm going to go home." To Cusick, I think. Cusick or Wellpinit [Washington]. I don't know just where. So, my mother went upstairs. She came down with — them days Pendleton blanket was kind of scarce. And she give this old man. He says, "What's that for?" Oh, she says, "Just to be friends. You helped Agnes." He says, "Oh, I thought you was paying me. I wasn't going to take it." He said, "I'm working myself up here." So, train used to go down towards Spokane about four o'clock in the afternoon. He says, "Well, I'm going." My dad said, "I'll go with you." So, they went. Got to the depot, and he was going to get himself ticket to Spokane. That guy got the ticket. My dad went to the window and said. "How much is it?" It used to be about six dollars. So, "What you doing that for? I was going to pay." "No, we're friends. When I go to your place, you have to do something for me." "Okay." So, he says, "Tell Agnes, I'll sit on that side. I'm going to wave at her." So, they told me to stand by the door. He took his scarf. He had a kind of green, red striped one. Got his scarf off and just waved.

Then, when I got alright, we happened to be over in Wellpinit. And they said this old man died. He had an Indian name. I don't know if he had family, or was just an old man.

Tom: I remember when you told me the story up at your camp, you described how it felt when you drank that medicine? How did it feel when you drank it?

Agnes: Well, cause I don't eat you know. That's all I could feel. Well, he told me, if you believe in that medicine, it'll help you. I told him, "I've been waiting since you left." So, "Okay." You notice when you drink something, even pop, not coffee, but something different. You don't feel it. That's what I did.

Tom: You feel it going in every part of you like that?

Agnes: So, I always thought I could cure that, if somebody come to me and tell me. I could try and help.

Tom: You knew the medicine that he gave you.

Agnes: Yea.

Tom: When he gave it to you, he just gave it to you like that, didn't do any . . .
Agnes: No, he said, "We have to pray." I knew, but my folks followed him, so we did. He said the first thing you have to do is pray, so we did.

Tom: Who do you pray to?

Agnes: God.

Tom: And how soon after he went back to Washington did he die?

Agnes: I don't remember just how long. I wasn't keeping track of the years, the months.

Tom: Years though after.

Agnes: Yea.

Tom: So, do you think there are people around who could cure people like that still?

Agnes: Yea.

Tom: I was wondering, was the tape being changed when I was asking her, "What would happen after the gas was gone?" That was right when the tape was being changed, wasn't it? Okay, I would like to ask that question again, because I want to get that one on tape. What do you think is going to happen when the gas is gone?

Agnes: I'll be glad.

Tom: What would people do?

Agnes: Go back to the horses. Just about no more horses. I got two. I'm okay.

Tom: You'll be safe, huh. Now let me think what else.

Other: Do you remember the day that the lights went on, when you got electricity? What was that like?

Agnes: Just kind of awful thing to go through. I really miss it too. It was off for four hours. Our stove, our light, my deep freeze, my refrigerator, everything. Sit there. I got five kerosene lamps. Just about had them all out there.

Tom: When was that?

Agnes: This winter sometime.

Tom: I think she was wondering, though, back in the forties, when they first got electricity in. She was asking what it was like when you first got electricity.

Agnes: Oh, I thought it was something good, you know. I really like it. This one old lady, they put electricity in her house. "Don't use kerosene, you might burn yourself. You might knock your kerosene lamp. She'll burn." So, they put in on for her. You start it like this, you open like this. When night came she forgot it. How was she going to turn the light off. She had a cane. She went and hit her bulb, and it went off.

There was all kinds of crazy stuff. Like me, I used to like to make jello. Before we had electricity, I put it under our little flue. I put it under the cupboard. And after I got electricity, I never did make any more. It's too easy.

Tom: It's not fun any more?

Agnes: It's kind of something new. But now everybody knows what they got. Like they always want electricity at my camp. I said, "No." I run away from here, you know, electricity bill, for four months. I don't want to be paying two places.

Tom: It's a good idea. Any time in your life, did you ever go down to the river much? Did you ever spend much time around the river? For any reason? Usually if you go camping it would be up in the mountains?

Agnes: Yea.

Tom: One question I was asking Agnes Kenmille, was if she knew any stories about spiritual things around the river. Anything like that? She told us that story about when her husband was killed down there. There were a lot of coyotes and owls that were trying to warn her about what was going to happen. She was only 19 or something, so she wasn't smart enough to hear what was being said.

Agnes: Yea, there a lot of way they could warn you. Even your own dog, or owl, coyote. Come out and give your dog a whipping for doing something, trying to warn you. "Shut up. Go lay down."

Tom: Dog was trying to warn you. Especially owls will say a lot of things that way.

Okay, anything else that comes to mind for you?

Other: Just that question that you mentioned about if the people on the reservation will make a lot of money [unintelligible].

Tom: That's a good one. This is a good one. What I was asking was, you know there is that new agreement with the power company, and they are going to get that nine million a year from the dam. And for the next thirty years that would come to a lot of money, two hundred and seventy million dollars. What do you think of that?

Agnes: I don't know. That's just like what they did, you know, Stevensville. It took about fifty years, maybe more than that before we got it. In thirty years, they'll go some more. It take quite a while.

Tom: What happened to all that money from Stevensville?

Agnes: Everybody got it. I didn't.

Tom: Why not?

Agnes: It went to my house. I signed my check, and they can have it.

Tom: So, it all went out in per capita payments? What did most people spend it on?

Agnes: Cars, I suppose. You see a lot of new cars.

Tom: And booze?

Agnes: Yea, there's were a lot of them went through. Jail, fine, and all that stuff.

Tom: Do you think that money could be spent on something good?

Agnes: If they could just do it, they could, but they won't. "That's not theirs, its mine. I'll do what I want to do with mine." That's what a lot of them say.

Tom: What do you think the money could be spent on? What would you like to see it spent on that would do some good?

Agnes: Spend it right. Cause one year is short. You should try and save it as long as you can have it, you know. You don't have to spend it in two days. Some they do.

Tom: You know the council has been talking different ideas for spending. Sometimes they say, "Oh, we should spend it on setting up new businesses." Sometimes they say, "No, we should spend it on per capita payments." Sometimes they say, "No, we should spend it on land. Buying land back. You know, the land that whites own now in the valley, buy that back." Some of them say, "No, we should spend it on the tribal college, education for the younger people." So, what do you think?

Agnes: Young people. Now I see that they are in their fifties trying to go to college. Why didn't they go to college right after they finished their high school. That's what I did to my kids. After they got a big family, then they want to go through college. They had a lot of time to put their four years in. They're done. But no, they want to get married, reach thirty or forty. They find out they done something wrong. After it's too late, then they go to college. That's where we spend all our money. Some they go to college, they don't even finish their college, they drop. Some they do finish it, but where are they are too old to get hired in some office or someplace.

Coming Back Slow

by Agnes Vanderburg

*Agnes Vanderburg is a venerated member of a distinguished family of Flathead Indian tribal leaders. The old ways of doing, which are also ways of being, are part and parcel of what she is: a simple, non-nonsense, working model of a just exchange between the human being and the powers that rule his universe. Mrs. Vanderburg passes on her knowledge of these ways of being-doing to the children (the ones who will listen) at St. Ignatius and other schools, and in summer at her camp on the reservation, not far from Arlee, Montana, to anyone of any age who wishes to come and learn. **Parabola** asked her to tell us what she thinks about old people and old ways, and why they are important.*

Well, when I grew up, things were different. In my time there was a lot of berries, a lot of game, fish, everything. But now everything is gone — the roots, the berries. That is what I see: they don't grow no more. The reason why is because when they are ripe, nobody prays when they grab the berries to put 'em in their mouth; they just go in there and eat off the bushes. It's the same with the roots. The oldtimers believed they had to pray for everything before they tasted it. But now, they don't believe in anything anymore. I tell my kids: I'm getting there, this February fourteenth I'll be seventy-nine; so I know a little bit about what's behind me. So I tell them: do what I was taught; then when I've gone, you'll know whatever I knew. But now you believe in the other way, you don't believe in our Indian ways.

I always tell my kids I am ready any time. I did everything with my two hands. I'm ready. I should be laying down taking rest. When you get too old, you don't use your hands no more. One of your kids has to take care of you. Some old people can't walk, they are hard of hearing or blind. But you have to take care of your elders after they get that old. You can't just put them in an old people's home and forget about them. You're supposed to pay them for what they did for you from the time you were born. That's the way we do; we take care of our elders, we don't put them in an old people's home, even if they can't walk or talk.

In the old days, when the people were moving from place to place, they took the old people with them. Lots of different places they're buried. If they were on their travels when they died, they buried them right there.

Now, I'm trying to teach people what I know about the old ways of doing things. I teach some at St. Ignatius, beading and quill work, like that. I see kids aren't interested in school. That's the reason why what they're doing is mostly in their heads. You see on TV what's going on. That's the way a lot of them learn how to do these bad things; they even show on TV how to steal a car, how to break into a house. They show you how to open the locks, how to open windows, how to destroy cars. That's what I don't like. That's where they learn all these bad things. They don't care to learn the good way from their teacher.

Then I have a camp, where I teach; I stay over there three months in the summer. I'll have it again next summer. I had five hundred and fifty-two kids — people — up there this year. (Anybody younger than me, I call 'em kids.)

Some stay a few hours, some ask if they could come again in a week or maybe tomorrow, so they can learn what I'm teaching. The longest they stay is two weeks. It's three years now I've done this. I go about four miles down the highway and turn left; I got all my signs on the road where everybody can see how to get to my camp.

When I came back I missed my camp. Everything seemed noisy. Over there it's still. That good water — there's kind of a spring that comes out of the ground.

Agnes Vanderburg
Courtesy Séliš–Qlispé Culture Committee,
St. Ignatius, Montana

One of the things I'm teaching them is how to make Indian saddles, because that's gone too; you don't see no Indian saddles anymore. You make your frame out of wood and cover it with wet rawhide, and sew it where it needs to be sewed. Then when it gets dry it kind of grabs the wood.

Yes, that's the thing: kids don't care to go to school. I had five; I made 'em all go all the way through, high school, college; then the three boys went in the service.

Even the language is gone. Just to be funny, I start talking Indian to these kids and they look at me and say, "I don't know what your're saying." They're starting in now teaching it again in the school here. But they call and ask me what this word means. I say: You're supposed to be teachers! You got to pay me five dollars for every word. They owe me a lot of money now! [laughs]

Sometimes I show 'em how to make the sign language — you see, Indians, they can't keep their hands still; when they talk, their hands are going. That's part of the talking. People can understand the movements. [She demonstrates.] "You are talking: I hear you: what?" You see, you can pretty nearly understand just by the movements.

When I was growing up, everyone was talking Indian. So when I went to school at the Agency, it was okay to talk Indian there. But first thing I knew we had to go to St. Ignatius and there was nothing but English. Then when we'd get together and start talking Indian, we'd sure get scolded for that; they didn't want us to talk Indian. We got scared to talk. That's why a lot of Indians stopped talking their own language.

I've visited different tribes and it's the same; they just wanted to talk their own language. But all the tribes are different. The Nez Perce, for instance; you can't understand them. And the Kootenai — they talk fast. Even between here and St. Ignatius there's different words. So when the oldtimers get together we talk with sign language. We say: What kind of Indian are you? This is the way: we go like that [she shows a movement of right hand raised, then touching the back of her left hand].

Then there's what my grandparents said: When all Indians start taking one language, then you better watch it: the world's going to end. And I believe it, because they are all talking English now. But the old language is coming back slow — so they might stop it, if they try.

But some of the kids don't want to learn the Indian ways. That's what gets me mad. At Dixon School, they brought an elk and a deer to make jerky — that's what we call dried meat — so they laid it on a big table. The teacher say: Agnes, you show the girls how to slice it. One girl was just barely touching the knife and the meat. I went over to her, and I really grabbed her hand and made her hold the knife tight. I took her other hand and put it right on that meat. I says: Here, that's the way you do it; and I started cutting it, holding on to her hands. I made her touch the meat and grab that knife the way she should. Then I left. But the others started cutting when I showed them, and in no time I saw a bunch of meat on the rack.

Some, I just call them bullheaded. If they don't want to do it they don't do it, and I tell them: Well, you get away from here, then! If you want to be bullheaded I'll be bullheaded too; go on! I want to teach everybody the old ways, and that's what I was doing.

But nobody has any more berries stored for the winter, no roots, nothing; there are no berries any more. It's been about three years there are no huckleberries. What I always tell them: Do what we're supposed to do, it will come back. The water's going really dry, the lakes went way down. It's because they don't believe in anything anymore. The way the old people was, they never had no doctors, and now everybody's going to doctors. They knew what the roots and plants were for. Now there's all sorts of sickness, heart attacks, cancer, all that stuff; we've got the medicine for 'em, if they'd just leave these drugs and pills and shots; that's no good for your body. I start showing them all our medicine. When you get them from the ground, or off the tree, you can't just go over there and dig 'em out; when you find them, you got to take something you really like, and talk to this plant and tell him what you're going to do with it, and then bury what you are offering in the ground. Then you dig the root or whatever you need, and then that helps.

There's a place the other side of Hamilton where we've got a medicine tree. This tribe used to believe in that tree. Every fall and every spring they'd go over there. They went over there to give that tree a present. Whatever they wish for they tell that tree. You know the story? Well, they say that once a great big mountain sheep was chasing Coyote, and Coyote, he was running for his life, and he came to this tree and got behind it. The sheep charged right into the tree and rammed one of his horns in the tree and got stuck there. So Coyote said: Now this tree will be the medicine tree, and whoever comes to pray to this tree, he got to give it a payment and he can ask for anything he wants.

Just about a month ago I took some people over there. I told them: Don't just come here and laugh; you got to pay this tree. Whatever you want to be, anything you want, you tell him, but you got to pay this tree. This tree had a lot of these coins that people had stuck into it, old money, and later people came and cut into the tree so that there was a bunch of holes. You could tell where there used to be a dollar, a fifty-cent piece, or a quarter — it was just like a woodpecker had been chipping on that bark. One man, oh, he was mad; he says: Why didn't I know when I was young? I said: 'Cause you didn't care! What your old grandmother knew, you didn't care to know.

Last year and this year I took some people there. But our tree is dying from the top. They're saying it's on account of everybody taking things out of the tree. There's just a bunch of holes in the trunk, where people have taken the money out, because it's old money, old coins.

So there's another thing that's in our belief, that medicine tree.

There was one woman that when she got old enough to comb her hair, her mother says: Take care of the hair that comes

Agnes Vanderburg,
drawing by Kathy Roullier, Polson, Montana

off in your comb, keep it and this spring we'll take it back to the medicine tree, because I want you to have black hair no matter how old you are. So in the spring they go over there; she puts the hair in that tree, or else on the ground, and tells the tree: I want to have black hair no matter how old I am. So that's the way she was, her hair stayed black until she died.

It comes true if you make up your mind what you're going to tell that tree; but if you just go over there for a joke, nothing is going to help.

In my Grandma's time they went over there with their horses, and there was a hole in the tree where the mountain sheep put his horn in, and they put all their beads in that hole, or whatever they wanted to put in; but after all the oldtimers went, that hole closed over.

We still got the medicine tree, but there are no medicine men anymore. In their time they didn't have doctors; it was the spirit that came to them that cured all different sicknesses. There was one old man that cured even for babies. That's all they depended on, was the medicine men. But now if they tried to have medicine men, they would just try to go on what they heard about the way it was. But there aren't any, anymore. The old grandmothers used to say it's because we're living in a box — that means, in a house; and in those days, they were staying in tepees, so their spirit could come to them. But not the way we live now. That's why we are not strong like the old ancestors.

My Grandma died when she was a hundred and fourteen. My mother died when she was eighty-four. My grandfather — I didn't really know how old he was.

And I was with my husband fifty-three years when he died. Now kids get married and in two weeks they part. I say, you have got to face one person. But they can't.

I try to tell 'em what we left behind. Just teach 'em that. That's what I've been trying to do for three years now: tell 'em what's right and what's wrong — that's easy done. Sometimes you get angry and holler at 'em, but you have to tell 'em what's right and what's wrong. Some take your word and some don't;

it's okay. Tell 'em what you know of the old ways. A lot of 'em don't care, but some of them do. Why I'm doing this is because it used to be on my chest all the time. I like to tell everybody what I know and now that weight on my chest is gone. Then I feel good. So it is the way to do it. What little you know, tell 'em. You feel good afterward; you get everything right for yourself. And some of them will listen.

Source: Agnes Vanderburg, "Coming Back Slow," *Parabola: Myth and the Quest for Meaning*, vol. 5, no. 1 (February 1980), pages 20-23.

'Good power, good medicine' Mary Agnes Vanderburg, 1901-1989

by Ron Selden for the *Missoulian*

Arlee — While an irreplaceable piece of the past was lost last week with the death of Salish elder Mary Agnes Vanderburg, her tenacious spirit will guide others to continue teaching tribal traditions on the Flathead Reservation, friends and relatives say.

Vanderburg, 88, was pronounced dead Wednesday night in a Missoula hospital after being taken there by helicopter from her home south of Arlee.

Her life touched thousands of people who over the years visited her rustic camp southwest of Ravalli to learn how to tan hides, prepare wild foods, and find themselves in a world gone awry.

"In a lot of ways, she's like the heart of the reservation," said friend and former Salish and Kootenai Tribal Chairman Ron Therriault. "A lot of what she taught was how to be a human being. She had good power, good medicine. She was strong that way."

Born in the Jocko Valley area on Valentine's Day 1901, "Yaya" (Salish for "grandmother"), as she was affectionately known, spent most of her life learning and teaching the old ways of her people.

"Over the years, she kind of took all the Indians on the reservation under her wing," said her sister, Harriet Whitworth.

Agnes Vanderburg.
Photo taken by Clarence Woodcock.
Courtesy Séliš–Qlispé Culture Committee,
St. Ignatius, Montana

"She felt sorry for them. They were all groping for answers about their language and culture. She felt she could help."

For years before her husband's death, Agnes and Jerome Vanderburg conducted a teaching camp in the Little Prairie area east of Arlee. There, the couple received dozens of guests who wanted to learn more about Indian culture.

After her husband died, Vanderburg moved the camp to Valley Creek, near the northeast side of S...w Peak. Since the mid-1970s, she and other family members had spent the warmer months of the year living at the camp while they taught traditions to anyone who cared to enter.

"She wanted to pass on everything she knew," explained Germaine DuMontier, a longtime friend. "But I don't think it's so important that she taught people how to tan hides or do beadwork as all the wisdom she taught with it. She told us how to connect our lives."

"There are dozens of people who can teach us to tan hides," added tribal elder Charlie McDonald. "But the things she taught us about spirituality, a good heart, how to believe, these are the riches she gave us."

Described as a kind and gentle person who never harbored bitterness or prejudice, Vanderburg was especially known for her effective teaching methods.

"She wouldn't say you did something wrong, but she'd show you how to do it right," said Therriault, who has taken students from Salish Kootenai College in Pablo to the camp the past five years. "She had a lot of dignity that couldn't help but rub off on anyone who spent time with her."

As one of a dwindling number of full-blooded Indians left on the reservation, Vanderburg drew international attention in her later years. Her camp register, which friends say contains thousands of names, includes visitors from all over the world.

In 1984, the woman who never drank or drove took her first airplane ride. Her destination was Washington, D.C., where she had been invited to participate in the Festival of American

Folklife, an annual event sponsored by the National Park Service and the Smithsonian Institution.

While she couldn't read English and could barely write, Vanderburg shared her knowledge of tribal customs with hundreds of visitors on the National Mall in Washington. She also returned later to the nation's capital to take part in another of the folklife festivals.

Along with receiving a birthday card from the White House each year, Vanderburg in 1983 was given special recognition by former Gov. Ted Schwinden for her many cultural contributions. She also held an honorary degree from Salish Kootenai College and continued to be a consultant to the tribes on cultural affairs.

In recent years, the tribal council has allocated money to the camp to keep it operating. Even as her health was failing, Vanderburg anxiously had awaited her return to the camp for its scheduled opening this weekend.

Friends say she had one of her sons drive her to the Valley Creek area to have a look around on Wednesday evening. Her sister said she had spent the entire day visiting friends.

"She was getting tired," said Whitworth. "She said this was probably her last year. Indian people, they know when they're going to go."

After visiting her beloved camp in the mountains, Vanderburg returned home and went to bed.

It was the last thing she did.

Source: Ron Selden, "'Good power, good medicine,'" *Missoulian*, June 4, 1989, pages B1 and B2.

Mary Agnes Vanderburg

Arlee — Mary Agnes Vanderburg, 88, of Arlee, died of natural causes Wednesday, May 31, at St. Patrick Hospital.

Born Feb. 14, 1901, in the Valley Creek area near Arlee to Eneas and Adele Adams, she attended the Sisters of Charity School until stricken with tuberculosis in the sixth grade.

In August 1920, she married Jerome Stanislaus Vanderburg.

She was known for being an extensive cultural information teacher on the Flathead Indian Reservation, and worked at the University of Montana in Missoula for Native American programs, especially the Native American Studies department, for 13 years.

Mrs. Vanderburg received an honorary degree from Montana State University and special recognition from the Montana Historical Society. She was also active in the Folk Life Festival in Washington, D.C.

With her background and knowledge of Indian traditions, medicines and treatments, she started a summer cultural camp in Valley Creek area in the late 1960s. The camp became a yearly event that received worldwide recognition.

Survivors include three sons, Eneas Raymond, Joseph and Victor, all of Arlee; two daughters, Anna Hazel and Lucy, both of Arlee; a sister, Harriet A. Whitworth, Arlee; 12 grandchildren, 12 great-grandchildren and one great-great-grandchild.

Traditional wake services began Friday at the St. Ignatius Community Center. Rosary will be recited 8 p.m. Sunday at the center; Mass of the Resurrection will be 10 a.m. Monday at the Jocko Catholic Church near Arlee, with the Rev. Joe Retzel as celebrant. Burial will be at Jocko Catholic cemetery. Arrangements are under the direction of the Fearon-Riddle Chapel of St. Ignatius.

Pallbearers are Eneas Raymond Vanderburg, Joseph Vanderburg, Joe Sequoyah Vanderburg, Victor Vanderburg, George Ernest Vanderburg and Barry Scott Vanderburg. Honorary pallbearers are Louie Adams, Mike Dempsey, Floyd Nicola, Tom Smith, Jim Dempsey and Gordon Sloan.

Source: "Mary Agnes Vanderburg," *Missoulian*, June 4, 1989, page B6.

Index